The Length
of a Clenched Fist

poems by

L A Felleman

Finishing Line Press
Georgetown, Kentucky

The Length
of a Clenched Fist

"Anyone who has shaved off or cut his beard will be imprisoned until the beard has grown to the length of a clenched fist."

The Bookseller of Kabul

Copyright © 2022 by L A Felleman
ISBN 978-1-64662-966-4 First Edition
All rights reserved under International and Pan-American Copyright Conventions. No part of this book may be reproduced in any manner whatsoever without written permission from the publisher, except in the case of brief quotations embodied in critical articles and reviews.

ACKNOWLEDGMENTS

With gratitude to the editors of the following who gave early versions of these poems a home:

Excerpts from "While Italians Sing Arias From Balconies," in *Lockdown Literature; Musings During a Time of Pandemic*; *Across the Social Distances*; and *Iowa City Poetry in Public*
"Cardinal Rules," *Global Poemic*
"How It Ends," *Art in the Time of COVID-19*
"I Remember Walking To Work," *Across the Social Distances*
"Sunken," *I Can't Breathe: A Poetic Anthology of Social Justice*
"Ill-Shod," *These Interesting Times*
"Curving Towards an Apex," *Lockdown 2020*
"Forsook," *Word Pond*
"We Can't Share Food, So I Thought: Flowers" *Backchannels Journal*
"Sei Shōnagon Judges Best In Show," in *Arriving at a Shoreline*, great weather for MEDIA

Publisher: Leah Huete de Maines
Editor: Christen Kincaid
Cover Art: *Grus grus* by Antonio Sales Martinez
Author Photo: Holly Lauer
Cover Design: Elizabeth Maines McCleavy

Order online: www.finishinglinepress.com
also available on amazon.com

Author inquiries and mail orders:
Finishing Line Press
PO Box 1626
Georgetown, Kentucky 40324
USA

Table of Contents

March
    While Italians Sing Arias from Balconies 1

April
    Mismanaged 9
    Cardinal Rules 10
    How It Ends 11

May
    The Bear Shall Lie Down With the Wolf 12
    I Remember Walking To Work 13
    Plagued 14
    Favored Things 15

June
    Sunken 16
    Ill-Shod 17
    Curving Towards an Apex 18

July
    Sei Shōnagon Judges Best in Show 19
    Immune 20
    2 bds. 1.5 ba 21
    The Tour 22

August
    Forsook 23
    Electricity Inequity 24
    Number One with a Bullet 25

September
    Modulation 26
    After-Supper Constitutional 27
    We Can't Share Food, So I Thought: Flowers 28

October
    Returning Sister Julie's Jelly Jar 29

March

While Italians Sing Arias from Balconies

*

Snowdrops poke through unraked clumps
If I am feeling ambitious
I could clear room for them
You point out suggestively

How am I feeling?

You gauge your symptoms
By my general state of being
Unsure if the common bugs you
Or something more novel
Like my gateway drink

Which okay sure, it resembles urine
But the taste was milder than the crude ones
Tried and rejected as a teen
Complementing my craving to be
Un-Midwestern-like

Tonight, you alter our bedtime routine
Pressing soft lips soundly
To the center of my forehead
Putting social distance between us

**
the kitchen calendar
is a series of squares
events struck through
on the inside

***
My sister quarantines our parents
Still, they slip through the church's side door
"We sat in the first pew," they promise
"We left before greeting anyone."

When Dad was young, he trained his lungs to run
Pushing asthma 'round the track 'til it collapsed
"He has three of the risks," Mom lists matter-of-factly
"Don't forget old," Dad chimes in trying to lift me

My sister's business trips are canceled
My niece's freshman year is canceled
My nephew's golf season is canceled
Church is canceled for the foreseeable Easter

****
soothed by repetitive
back and forth of sweeper
over hardwood floorboards
if only i had more

*****
Fitness centers are closed and they
Drive through windows grabbing local
Takeout each day like it contains
Their full patriotic duty

will i recognize anyone
after?

******

massaging in hair super cream
rather than usual lite brand
hoping extra conditioner
tames fly-away thoughts

****
Calmed by repetitive
Trilling call of Sandhills
Over Crane Cam live feed

We were supposed to be there in person
At sundown when they lifted from cornfields
Thousands swirling seeking shelter below

Congregating to the river safe
In their numbers

Remember sharing the instinct of social creatures?

****

friday fell on a thirteenth this year
that evening i spotted the first robin of Spring
those omens cancel each other out
true?

April

Mismanaged

The Facebook pics of every meal you ever cooked
While in quarantine
Offend my sensibilities

Equally so, that woman behind me
In the pink sweatshirt
Decorated with drooping daffodils
Who could not grasp the concept
Of keeping inside the square
Marked out in masking tape
Before the checkout lane

Let it be known that, while I have prayed over this attitude
The requested upgrade
Has yet to materialize
So really we can only blame our
Father, Son, and Holy Ghost
For being slow to respond
To this crisis

Cardinal Rules

Familiar whimper
Same sound I made when
the candidate I caucused for dropped out

Also uttered upon comparing the inanity
To what could have been
Whenever his opponent tweeted up

There are those who can manufacture profits
Even when all the buyers have gone home

There are others who run themselves florid
Organizing goods to keep them shelved

Outside the upstairs window
Cardinals fight over mating rights
To my backyard

Wish I could tell both crews what I think of them
Face to face

How It Ends

In the Cecil B. DeMille version
    we avert our gazes as Glory descends
    enemies fall to the floor
    succumbed into nothing

In the Broadway musical adaptation version
    your solo sounds surprisingly strong
    for a consumptive

In the Disney version
    I raise you with the obligatory chaste kiss

In this the Hospice version
    an iPod shuffles through your *Songs To Die By* playlist
    I sit beside you directing all things towards dignity
    our tears and final gratitudes are their
    best versions of themselves

    Until the morning, as the first robin
    challenges the dim haze
    to bloom beyond the horizon

    Then your laboring ceases
    Then I bless the day that sees you
    Release into freedom

May

The Bear Shall Lie Down With The Wolf

At the small of my back is a pillow
Belonging to one of our landlord's kids

Its pillowcase is white with green creatures
Bears with U's for eyes, U's at the end of their
      upside-down, triangular muzzles
Wolves with spikes for teeth, ears, and tails
      muzzles topped by ill-matched, bulbous noses

The bears are restful, comfy, downy-like
The wolves are pointed pikes, jagged daggers

Does this combination make for troubled
      childhood sleep, or
Does its yin and yang hold dreamers steady?
      I wonder

Contained above my head is a jumble
competing obligations pressed for time:
blue highlighters next to magic markers
used college texts beside kids' bedtime books
      shelved accordingly as to-dos unspooled

Don't we feel imposed on surrounded by
      artifacts of absentee owners?
Others ask us

I adjust until the bear-wolf pillow
Completely fills the gap between my back
The back of the landlord's corner chair
Surveying the scene of a stranger's space
Settle into the cushion of my home

I Remember Walking To Work

My neighbor's newspaper delivery man was usually
the first to greet me

I would lift a hand; smile
He would lean towards me; wave through his windshield

Crossing a windy bridge
Worrying over the spot where I slipped and sprained my wrist
Commuters braking in parallel below

Along a rise of brick apartment buildings
Sounds of water flowing through faucets
Windows cracked to vent shower steam

Around the VA bus stop
The VA smokers, patients and staff
Circling a common can

Down a steep slope to the traffic loop
Winding through the steady flow of those disembarking
Angling sharply up to the health campus complex crowning the hill

Past sparsely-filled bike racks in a back alley
Opening a door that requires a pass
Always that sense of belonging when the lock light turned green

Plagued

> And I said, "Lord, stop.
> Who will rescue Jacob?
> He is so small"
>   Amos 7:5

Bats drawing the blood
of cattle
in the Amazon.
The occupiers fear the harm
they will cause
to their livestock.
The harm they will cause
to their livelihood.
The drinking down to the bone bereft of blood
blood that forced life
into their valley
where they dwell
to fragile livings
in the jungle
in the rainforest
of the Amazon.
One of multitudes of creatures
a small animal
mammal in the whole and
what can occupiers do?
They do not fly
They cannot subsist on blood alone
or sunlight alone
or water and dirt nutrients.
They do not have fangs
or claws
or jaws to break bones
or a roar that threatens and cowers.

Little owner of vampire-bat-lapped herd
how will you defend yourself?
Protect yourself from the night things
of the rains
of the forests
of the vampires
subtly affixed

How will you protect you and yours?

Favored Things

Kathleen leashes her privilege
clips it in a cute, pink collar
walks it in early to its appointment
a shampoo, cut, and fluffing
probably bows will be administered
Who's Mommy's pretty baby?

Lathum hugs his privilege secure to him
clutches it in a fist against his breast
pulls it tight across his shoulders
relishing its warmth
Who's Daddy's snuggly baby?

Morgen gets her privilege season tickets
swipes her Platinum American Express
buyer protection on every purchase
not that she needs it
Who's Mommy's savvy baby?

Basal salutes his privilege with a latte
drinks to its good health at Gloria Jean's
orders it a triple mocha frappuccino
chocolate sprinkles topping whipped cream
Who's Daddy's classy baby?

Mary-Rose rolls her privilege through the market
its short legs banging against the cart
asks to see the manager when she has trouble
locating fair trade, organic, heirloom wild rice
Who's Mommy's hardy baby?

Alec lets his privilege take shotgun
lowers the window so it can stick its nose in the wind
ears streamlining around its head in pleasure
W.P. is my Co-Pilot bumping next to *Coexist*
Who's Daddy's happy, happy baby?

June

Sunken

The main garden dwells below street level
In a depression at 27th & Capitol
Conceived in 1930 as a make-work project
By Lincoln's city fathers

> Questions: Which one of the fathers gazed on the
> neighborhood dumping ground and imaged
> swapping in its opposite? What circumstances
> blind eyes to the real and instead favor potentiality?
> How much capital must a person have behind his
> name before his schemes become civic
> planning rather than childish irrationalities?

Out-of-luck men were paid $6.40 per week
To garden two eight-hour shifts in the winter
Removing trash and reassembling rocks
To evoke an English mountain scene in the prairie

> Questions: Which neighborhood inherited the
depression's trash? Where did the garden's
> neighbors dispose of their waste after their dumpsite
was repurposed? Did their castoffs mound in
> the edges of their yards or in the cobwebbed corners
of their basements? At some time in their
> former fortunes, had any of the unlucky gardeners ever
enjoyed the mountains?

The following Spring, the upper garden mimicked that of Sissinghurst Castle
White turtlehead, white foxglove, white iris, white caladiums, white nicotiana
White blossoms to glow in moonlight
White blossoms to release ethereal, healing calm

> Questions: What if white isn't your color? What if your
> wisdom teaches white equals blight? What other
> color could you go to for healing? What varieties
> would you plant to restore calm? What if, by the
> light of the moon, you become suspect? Where and
> when would you locate an alternate otherworldly?

Ill-Shod

Realizing a block from the house
what she was still wearing

Swim sandals promising
nonchalant walking of edges

Offering the privilege of being
unafraid of tidal reach

Doubtlessly designed by somebody facing
her kind of hard choices

White soles burning on white sands or
soggy soles sprouting mold in refrigerated conditions

A world beach traverser who imagined
producing a better third

Marketed to those who could envision
saltwater sliding under their untroubled arches

Never dreaming of this predicament
pulling into the parking lot stall

Pinching the yellow mask closer to her bridge
pulling the shield's elastic over her head

Resigning to be that shopper in inadequate footwear
the one her husband privately scorns

Noting the plywood-protected windows, she exits the car
leaves on the white footies

There's a chill to the day

Curving Towards An Apex

He does not have a lucky number
Every number is lucky for him

He does not have a favorite color
Every color holds favor for him

He does not have a person preference
Every person is exponential

Today

July

Sei Shōnagon Judges Best In Show
after the Pillow Book

Best is perfectly exemplifying

: manes ought to have the shine of mulberry threads
: lips must contain the gleam of pumice stone sand
: nails should hold the glow of cabbage moth wings

Best is pristinely expressing

: minds the white of rural beadboard homes
: hearts the white of royal brocade robes
: visions the white of whales' beached bones

Best is purely exuding

: offspring like cotton bolls bursting their bracts
  seeds protected by layered calyx
  cleanly soaked in lye-filled vats

Supreme among these shall be the extreme
best purged to a fragile pale glint

Immune

All night the wind made its presence heard
Scratching at shingles above her sleep
Herding leaves that now swirl at her heels

She does not seem concerned by the fact
Striding quick, clipped step to office work
Wrapped in the tart of Braeburn apples

She can ignore what circles behind
Given all she values has been saved
Pressing restart cannot injure hers

2 bds. 1.5 ba

His wife died last month
They keep reminding each other
When he adds hoops to the hurdles they've cleared

She was the one who handled the house
Loved learning about her new renters
He doesn't know how she did it

What date and time would work best for them?
His social calendar is empty
Would they mind sending him a reminder?

He's planning her funeral
Will get back to them tomorrow
Their credit looks good he guesses

His familiar flew apart when she passed
They reason that's why they don't have a lease
It isn't because they don't look like his kind

The Tour

Beginning in back with the scaly yellow paint
Of the loosely, screened-in porch
Which he planned to repair that Spring.

In the basement half-bath sat the new toilet still
In its dusty factory box
Which he planned to install that Fall.

Also on the list, the ceiling fan hanging
Above the living room couch
Which made a whirred whine it really shouldn't.

The musty A/C had been flagged on inspection
For its cracking power cord
He supposed it ought to be replaced.

He failed to point out the roof disrepair
The leak behind the built-ins
The black rot held up by clear tape.

He is resolved to make every amend
In no time.

August

Forsook

> *and the rain came down, and the rivers rose,*
> *and the wind blew and they struck against*
> *that house, and it fell*
> *and great was its downfall*
> *Matthew 7:27*

Emerging from shelters
Dazed by sun following storm
Finding messages beaded
In every West-facing window screen
Braille-shaped rain droplets reading
"Condolences on your loss"

Electricity Inequity

He is Shrug-of-the-shoulder-I'm-not-sure-When-was-that?
Tries raising his arms up over his head

Maybe airing out his graying blonde armpit hairs
Will help him remember what has been blacked out

As if he hadn't eaten all of the cherry vanilla non-fat yogurt
In the 32 oz container before it went bad

Sniff-tested the tofu and the pasta sauce
then proceeded to eat them for dinner

Ate bran cereal without milk this morning
Drank yesterday's bitter coffee without milk

Had canned black beans and canned white corn for lunch
Seasoned with cumin, but no splash of orange juice

Damn he had missed that citrusy tang

How long had it been since he'd flipped on the switch
Listened to the motor's effort as it lifted the door

Turned on the hum of the oscillating fan
Logged into the strong signal of his home network

Sat shirtless at the back of his well-swept garage
On a gray folding chair with thin, tilting legs

Watched neighbors from the downed power pole next door
walk by in envy?

Number One With A Bullet

A hurricane with my name on it made land fall
Also houses, apartment buildings, and churches
But not many mosques because
This is god's country
Sang Blake Shelton in his
Red-dirt-dusted skid-steer loader
Heart racing the motor as he claimed
His next certified gold standard because
In this god's country
Celebrity has hit after hit downloaded on it
While unknown is lowered by blows
Decisive and discriminate

September

Modulation

He is blocking her way.
He, the essential worker, is blocking her way.
Her way forward and out is blocked by him.
The worker, essentially gathering groceries for a remote shopper, is in her way.
He is blocking the end of the cereal aisle.
His cart is sideways across the end of the cereal aisle.
He is consulting his handheld searching for a remote order.
It is 5:00 AM on a Saturday.
He is of one tribe.
She is of another.
They have American history between them.
I need to be seen as one of the tolerant.
She needs him to move his cart to the right.
She needs him to stand behind his cart while his back is turned towards her.
She needs to roll past him on the left while holding her breath.
I am reluctant to face others' exhales.
She sighs, "They seem to be hiding the Grape Nuts."
He is instantly to her aid, the remote dropped.
"The Grape Nuts?" he voices.
Something inside her cringes.
He is walking towards her searching.
She is turning away, backing away from him pretending to be searching.
His voice is walking down passages towards her the long way.
The sound of his walk echoing through long passages is a cringe.
The cringe his voice makes makes her want to block her hearing.
Something inside her finds the cringe in his voice aesthetically unpleasing.
She checks the cringing something inside her.
As if I am the newest judge on The Voice or something?
Once he is at a sufficient distance searching amongst the boxes,
she rolls her cart past his and grabs the Grape Nuts he had been blocking.
"Found it!" she shows him tolerantly while simultaneously rolling forward and out,
twisting a glance back, needing to show him the smile blocked behind her mask.

After-Supper Constitutional

Authorities do not patrol the non-perpetual care cemetery
bordering the city's Northern limits.
Cut flowers are left there to die.
Dogs are supposed to remain leashed, but
everybody ignores that fact
feeling it would be cruel to deny
Goldens or Huskies or Toys the chance to flex flat out in the empty.
Hilltop vistas were claimed centuries ago by
individual city pillars
judges, politicians, capitalists of the past
known now as the names on shunned mausoleums.
Lately, headstones of a common aesthetic have sprouted in the dells
marbles in various black hues etched with portraits of chiseled smiles.
Near the deeded body memorial beside the West exit
one tree snapped in half during the August storm
propped up by brokenness, the trunk
quests through grounded branches
reaching out to graves barely beyond its grasp
supplicant to whatever heavens trees believe in.
Tiny solar panels power angel-shaped night lights that
undulate from red to blue like dots of carnival in the gloaming.
Vines twist into second barks
weakening the host at the same time making it seem stronger.
Xenia is buried here. One of the faceless, white markers may be Xavier's.
Yesterday, we spotted a fox limping the fence line as we turned for home
zigzagging past droppings and deer that stared at our passage indifferently.

We Can't Share Food, So I Thought: Flowers

Six pink roses from her garden clustered
cut stems submerged in jelly jar labeled
From Julie's Kitchen: A Taste of Summer.
She centered the impromptu vase on the porch table
where she sat masked without shield
fogging up from the drizzle.
I remained shielded.
That hour, my visual cortex tried to assemble its view
shifting features blurred by droplets into a familiar
finally imposing the form of a Chinese dragon.
The dragon and I gossip over details
viruses, vaccines, victories
wetland trails, wildfire flares, whimsies
then the dragon left for her den; leaving the flowers
requested the jelly jar's return (a gift from her sister).
It stayed on my desk unfaded for two weeks
until the smell turned a saturated sweet.
The compost pile, mostly browns and slimes
is now rosy.

October

Returning Sister Julie's Jelly Jar

We will walk looping wetland trails
"Maybe we will see them," she will hope
I will tell her that I feel lucky
We will walk another loop
She will lift a hand to still my story
Our eyes will meet over our masks
Hers burgundy cloth with cream swirl patterns
Mine sky blue, paper, behind a black gator
I will see three sandhill cranes flying
We will move another loop closer
I will hear their trill in the tallgrass
She will hear their trill beyond the ridge
After filling up on trilling, we will loop for home
They will fly past, the three of them, at a distance
Remember having an instinct for social creatures?

Currently, **LA Felleman** is an accountant at the University of Iowa (MAcc, University of Nebraska, Omaha). Prior to that she was a seminary professor, and before that she was a pastor. She earned her PhD at Drew University, and her DMin and MDiv at Saint Paul of School of Theology.

She has published numerous scholarly articles and book chapters on Wesleyan theology and Methodist history. Her book chapter, "Having Received I Ought to Give: The impact of Hwa Nan College on Chinese Women," in *The Global Impact of the Wesleyan Traditions and Their Related Movements* (Scarecrow Press) received the 2001 Women in United Methodist History Writing Award. *The Form and Power of Religion: John Wesley on Methodist Vitality* (Wipf & Stock Press) was her first book.

She moved to Iowa City with her husband in 2016, and began writing poetry soon after settling in this UNESCO City of Literature. She has benefitted from the opportunity to interact with poets from all over the world who are drawn to this Midwestern college town by the Writers' Workshop and the International Writing Program. The local Free Generative Writing Workshops and Iowa City Poetry workshops have been particularly influential on her development as a poet.

Her poetry has appeared in *Hawai'i Review, Tiferet*, and *St. Katherine Review* among others, as well as in anthologies published in the United States, England, India, Kenya, and Australia. Her poems also have been included in the Texas Poetry Calendar, the Telepoem art installation (Iowa exhibit). and the Iowa City Poetry in Public program.

After noting how much participating in open mics and the community IHearIC concert series helped her hear what was and what was not working in her poems, LA organized an open mic at the local library to encourage other beginning writers to share their work in public. The Writers Open Mic launched in 2017 and continues on Zoom during the COVID-19 pandemic.

Her other community involvements include serving on the advisory council of Iowa City Poetry, as well as on the board of directors of the Wesley Center, a campus ministry at the University of Iowa.

This is her first chapbook.

www.ingramcontent.com/pod-product-compliance
Lightning Source LLC
LaVergne TN
LVHW041509070426
835507LV00012B/1435